The Greatest Liar on Earth

A True Story

Mark Greenwood

illustrated by Frané Lessac

CANDLEWICK PRESS

On account of a total eclipse, the dock was shrouded in darkness when the tramp descended the plank. He raised the collar of his shabby coat and set off into the London fog with a plan that would assure him fame and fortune.

He made his way to the British Museum.
There, he studied explorers' diaries and travelers' tales and spun a fabulous yarn. He filled the grimy pages of a notebook with his elaborate scrawl about how he had returned from the edge of the known world with the most amazing story any man had ever lived to tell.

This masterpiece, *The Adventures of Louis de Rougemont*, was published in a series of illustrated episodes. It was a breathtaking tale of catastrophe and miraculous events that astounded England's scientific minds. The author's celebrity grew with each gripping installment. He traded his shabby overcoat for a suit and was named "The Most Remarkable Man of the Century."

"It seems I have become quite famous!" he exclaimed.

The author was invited to deliver a series of lectures.
Outside, those without tickets set ladders against walls
and pressed their ears to the windows. Inside, there was
not a stir or a whisper when the adventurer stepped onto
the stage and recounted his astonishing experiences.

"On an expedition seeking rare black pearls, my greatest fear was a monster with enormous tentacles that could suck an entire boat down into the depths. I once witnessed a pearl diver vanish into the hideous cavity of its mouth."

The audience burst into spontaneous applause.

Louis raised a hand to silence the crowd. "In uncharted waters, my schooner drifted through heaving seas, where gruesome fish with bulging eyes and hairy mustaches reared out of the water."

A member of the Royal Geographical Society identified himself. "Is everything you say true?" he asked.

Louis smiled serenely. "Every word," he replied without hesitation.

"My ship met its doom on a pinnacle of coral," he said. "I was swept overboard by a freak mountain of water. Bruno, the ship's dog, saved my life. I took his tail between my teeth, and that brave hound tugged me, half drowned, onto a lonely spit of sand."

"I survived on evening dew and fish emptied from pelicans' pouches and vowed that my bones would not be added to the grisly remains of sun-bleached skeletons. To cast aside my melancholy, I taught Bruno acrobatic tricks and rode sea turtles, steering left or right by covering their eyes with my toes."

"A turtle gondolier!" joked a heckler.

"It was as I've said," Louis replied. His conviction was indisputable.

The audience roared its approval. Louis waved triumphantly.

At the conclusion of each lecture, Louis celebrated his fame at fancy restaurants.

A perfect likeness of him was crafted from wax and displayed at Madame Tussauds.

He was even summoned to the royal palace for
an audience with the queen of England.

"Tell me, monsieur," asked the queen, "is it true
you wrestled a crocodile?"

"I ran straight up to the great brute," Louis replied, "leaped onto its scaly back, and thrust my paddle into its vicious jaws. I wear six of the reptile's razor-sharp teeth around my neck."

At the height of his fame, newspaper reporters began to investigate Louis's identity. Evening editions declared him an impostor whose real name was Henri Grin.

But Louis simply expressed surprise that his story could be doubted. "I will leave it to the public to judge me," he said.

Despite his critics, the lines to witness Louis in action grew longer. Each SOLD OUT sign inspired him to tell more marvelous adventures. At one lecture, the Association for the Advancement of Science greeted him with a rousing ovation.

"After two years on the deserted isle," Louis said, "I cast off from that cruel shore on a rickety platform of logs. Bruno and I drifted at the mercy of the sea for fifteen days and nights before a sliver of land appeared. Imagine my horror when cannibals brandishing barbed spears rushed to the shore. Terrified that they might boil me in a pot and eat me, I played a tune on a reed whistle. Bruno danced on his hind legs and performed acrobatics. With great merriment, the fearsome clan threw down their weapons and placed themselves at my disposal.

"At dusk, flying wombats rose in great clouds," Louis said.

"Preposterous," muttered a disbeliever.

"Truth is sometimes stranger than fiction," Louis remarked, ignoring jeers and hisses.

"On my desperate search for civilization, I trekked through parched deserts. I battled swarming bull ants with stings that can kill and survived in a pit of black snakes."

Louis raised his hands to silence murmurs of disbelief that rippled through the theater. "I witnessed rainstorms in which fish fell flapping from the clouds."

Cynics shook their heads and called him a master of
beautiful lies.

"I discovered nuggets of gold too big for one man to carry,"
he continued, "and mountains of blood-red rubies."

"You have a gift for rip-roaring tales," muttered a critic.

"I witnessed a plague of rats so thick that they formed a living bridge that spanned a lagoon. The murky water was home to an evil monster that carried a deadly sword in its mouth. The dreaded creature charged me and thrashed about, piercing both sides of my canoe."

Calls of "Liar!" grew louder.

"Do not think I am discourteous," Louis begged
the restless crowd, "but I am obliged to decline
questions." He departed the stage to the thunder
of boos and stamping feet.

Newspaper headlines declared *The Adventures of Louis de Rougemont* to be the concoction of a charlatan. The author's reputation was shattered. His lectures struggled to draw crowds.

Louis took his exposure with arctic coolness. His fame could be revived, he believed, with a new plan—a vaudeville act, billed as "The Greatest Liar on Earth."

But howls of mocking laughter greeted his reappearance onstage. Before he even began his story, cries of "Trickster!" and "Liar!" took hold. He struggled to be heard above the heckling.

Illuminated by the dim rays of gaslight, the forlorn traveler hung his head. "Who has not walked in the woods, seen a cat, and called it a wolf?" he asked.

He marked his exit from the stage with a modest wave.

His finale took place many years later.

"It's him," whispered a newsboy.

A stooping figure stood shivering in the snow, selling books of matches in Piccadilly Circus. "Throughout my life, I have suffered misfortune," he said. "But people here are more vicious than they are in the wilds. They robbed me of fame and fortune. They follow me in the streets and laugh at me."

The Greatest Liar on Earth adjusted the collar of his ragged coat
and marked the moment with a theatrical bow. Then, like a ghost,
he vanished into the London fog.

THE AMAZING ADVENTURES OF LOUIS DE ROUGEMONT

Louis de Rougemont (1847-1921) was a real person who was born Henri Louis Grin. He claimed to have traveled in and around Australia performing amazing feats and witnessing amazing things. Could these events possibly be true? Was de Rougemont the most remarkable explorer of the century or was he the greatest liar on earth?

Riding Turtles—Believe It or Not

De Rougemont claimed to have ridden turtles, but skeptics declared him a "master of beautiful lies."

In the summer of 1906, an old man appeared at London's Hippodrome Arena to demonstrate turtle riding. He climbed onto the back of a large turtle. Covering its eyes with his toes, he steered the creature to the center of a large water tank and back. In a dripping bathing costume, Louis de Rougemont stood at the edge of the arena and delivered a triumphant bow.

Monsters of the Deep— Truth Is Stranger than Fiction

Was de Rougemont a clever charlatan, or did he really witness a hideous creature?

Giant squids have a long, torpedo-shaped body and a beak strong enough to cut through steel cables. Their two long tentacles, used for catching prey, can be as long as a school bus, and their eight arms each have swiveling hooks and suckers. Their eyes can grow as big as basketballs.

In 2007, fishermen caught a colossal squid near Antarctica. The mysterious creature weighed 990 pounds (450 kg) and measured 33 feet (10 m) in length.

Freak of Nature—
It's Raining Fish!

Critics scoffed at de Rougemont's tale of fish falling from the sky.

Next time the heavens open up, it may not be raindrops falling on your head. Raining fish is a weird weather phenomenon that can actually happen. When cold air moves over warm water, waterspouts can form that suck fish out of the ocean and into clouds that are then carried over land. In February 2010, hundreds of spangled perch fell from the skies onto the remote community of Lajamanu, on the edge of the Tanami Desert in the Northern Territory, Australia.

A Rip-Roaring Tale—
or a strange coincidence?

De Rougemont said the powerful winged birds he saw on his desolate island gave him an idea.

De Rougemont claimed to have scratched messages with a nail into the lids of condensed-milk cans and fastened them to pelican's necks with fish gut.

In 1887, five boys walking along a beach in Australia discovered a giant seabird with a tin disk fastened around its neck. The message, punched in by a nail, was written in French. The author professed to be shipwrecked.

Bruno—a faithful friend

Bruno was with Louis through all his sufferings. His companionship was the greatest blessing Louis knew. That brave hound watched over him when he was struck down with fever and had to sleep inside a dead buffalo until he was cured. When Louis talked to his dog, he was sure Bruno understood every word, but he claimed what delighted Bruno most was when Louis told him how much he loved him.

For Rusty

Special thanks to
Frank and Lyne Greenwood, Sue Whiting, Sarah Foster, and Marcia Wernick

The texts from the lectures in this book are an invention of the author,
paraphrased from *The Adventures of Louis de Rougement*, as well as other sources.

SOURCES:

Andrews, B. G. "de Rougemont, Louis (1847–1921)." In Vol. 8 of *Australian Dictionary of Biography*. Melbourne: Melbourne University Press, 1981.

Clune, Frank. *The Greatest Liar on Earth*. Melbourne: Hawthorn Press, 1945.

de Rougemont, Louis. *The Adventures of Louis de Rougemont*. London: George Newnes, 1899.

Howard, Rod. *The Fabulist*. Sydney: Random House, 2006.

Maslen, G. J. *The Most Amazing Story a Man Ever Lived to Tell*. Sydney: Angus and Robertson, 1977.

Text copyright © 2012 by Mark Greenwood
Illustrations copyright © 2012 by Frané Lessac

First U.S. edition 2012

Library of Congress Cataloging-in-Publication Data is available.

Library of Congress Catalog Card Number pending

ISBN 978-0-7636-6155-7

CCP 17 16 15 14 13 12

10 9 8 7 6 5 4 3 2 1

Printed in Shenzhen, Guangdong, China

This book was typeset in Goudy Old Style.
The illustrations were done in gouache.

Candlewick Press
99 Dover Street
Somerville, Massachusetts 02144

visit us at www.candlewick.com